The Sharp Family, Johann Zoffany, 1779. The painting is preserved in the National Portrait Gallery, and six of the instruments, the two horns by John Christopher Hofmaster, the two clarinets by George Miller, and the two one-hand flageolets by John Mason, in the Bate Collection of Historical Instruments, Oxford. All are lent by kind permission of C. M. G. Lloyd-Baker Esq.

THE FLUTE

Jeremy Montagu

Shire Publications Ltd

CONTENTS

Printed in Great Britain by C. I. Thomas & Sons (Haverfordwest) Ltd, Press Buildings, Merlins Bridge, Haverfordwest, Dyfed SA61 1XF.

British Library Cataloguing in Publication Data: Montagu, Jeremy. The flute. 1. Transverse flutes, history. I. Title. 788.32. ISBN 0-7478-0085-5.

Cover: *Katharine Bircher playing a silver Boehm system flute extended to low B flat by Eugène Albert, Brussels, mid nineteenth century. (Bate Collection 1090.)*

ACKNOWLEDGEMENTS
The author wishes to thank the Bate Collection of Historical Instruments, Faculty of Music, University of Oxford, for permission to use photographs of some of the flutes in the Collection. The frontispiece, which hangs in the National Portrait Gallery, London, is reproduced by kind permission of C. M. G. Lloyd-Baker Esq. The portrait of Charles Nicholson on page 16 hangs in Bodelwyddan Castle and is reproduced by courtesy of the National Portrait Gallery, London. Photographs are by Michael Bass.

The upper and lower body joints of an ivory flute by Thomas Cahusac, London, 1789, showing the differing sizes of the fingerholes. (Bate Collection x10.)

HOW FLUTES WORK

There are many varieties of flute in the world, but this book is concerned only with the type called the transverse flute or cross flute as it is used in Europe. This is a tube, nowadays usually made of metal but originally of wood or reed, stopped at one end and open at the other. It has a hole in the side close to the stopped end, across which the player blows to produce a sound. There are further holes between the blowing hole, or embouchure, which the player opens or closes with fingers or keys to obtain different notes.

This is a non-technical introduction to how flutes work; those interested in scientific acoustics should consult the books by Bate and Benade.

Flutes are sounded by a stream of air blown across an opening in the side of the tube so that the air stream eddies with regular pulsations, forcing the column of air within the tube to vibrate. We hear this vibration as musical sound. The basic pitch is controlled mainly by the length: the longer the flute, the lower the basic pitch, and the shorter the higher.

A flute can be overblown, by changing the angle and speed of the air stream, to sound higher harmonics. Thus players can play a scale by opening the fingerholes in succession, cover all the holes again, blow a little harder and play a scale an octave higher; correct fingering differs from one model of flute to the next.

Fingerholes depend greatly on their diameter for their effect. A hole the same diameter as the bore is so effective that it acts as though the tube were cut off at that point. A smaller hole is less effective and produces a lower pitch than a wider one in the same position. So a narrow hole 20 cm from the foot can produce the same pitch as a wider hole only 15 cm from the end. Thus the holes of the pre-Boehm flute were kept within the span of the hand.

The effect of the hole is also controlled by its shape. The inner end can be opened, or undercut, and so made effectively wider, while still being comfortably closed by the finger. Partly filling holes with wax reduces their diameter. The player can also shade a hole with the finger, partly covering it and thus reducing its effective diameter, just

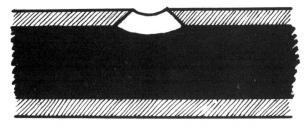

Drawing of a fingerhole with undercutting so that the end of the hole which meets the bore is wider than that covered by the finger, thus effectively widening the hole and raising the pitch produced by opening it. Most pre-Boehm flutes have some or all of their holes undercut.

as the embouchure, which is simply another of the holes, is shaded with the lip. Similarly, players of the old one-key flute cross-finger, closing holes below, for example, the B hole to produce B flat; cross-fingering reduces the area of open hole and therefore produces a lower pitch.

The bore shape is critical for the tuning. Every irregularity, every contraction or expansion, affects the tuning of all or some of the notes, and makers take advantage of this.

The bore diameter affects mainly the tone quality. A tube wide in proportion to its length has a stronger low register and a richer sound than a narrower tube but is difficult to overblow into the upper register; a narrow tube has a weak or thin fundamental but overblows easily. The diameter does have some effect on the pitch, but tone quality and ability to play in all registers are so important that makers choose a bore which best combines these features, which is why it was stated that the pitch is controlled mainly by the length, ignoring the diameter's influence.

The modern idea, the result of Boehm's keywork, is to place all the fingerholes where they will be in tune; formerly it was necessary to place them to lie under the hand, tune them as far as possible, and then leave it to the player to make them work. Because tuning can be controlled by fingering, it is misleading to pick up an old flute, play a scale by opening fingerholes in succession and then form any conclusions about its tuning. The tuning of any flute depends upon two people: the maker, who bored holes of a certain size in certain positions, and the player, who controls the resulting pitches by the mode of fingering and blowing found most effective. Thus an instrument by itself is little indication of the sort of sound it produced. Without the player, we have only half the evidence. When one plays the instrument, one begins to understand how it works.

In one of the earliest dated illustrations of flutes, a wood engraving by Hans Burgkmair in 1512 for The Triumph of Maximilian the Great, the fife players immediately precede five mounted side-drummers. Each of the fifers has, hanging from his belt, a case to hold four flutes, one small, two medium and one large.

4

THE MEDIEVAL AND RENAISSANCE FLUTE

Byzantine miniatures from the tenth century onwards show that the transverse or cross flute, which is held across the player's face, was common in the Eastern Empire, but there is little evidence for it in the rest of Europe for several centuries. In medieval and early renaissance times the common flute was the recorder. In Western Europe the transverse flute was first widely used in the late fifteenth century as the soldier's fife. The Swiss mercenaries, who fought in all the European armies, were mainly responsible for spreading its use; indeed it was often known as the Swiss pipe.

The best flutes came from Italy. They were made in one piece of wood, except for the bass, which was usually in two pieces, and were cylindrical in bore. The fingerholes were all about the same diameter and were in two groups of three, with a larger gap between each group than between each hole; the embouchure, into which the player blows, was usually small. Little is known of their musical use in the sixteenth century. Fifes were used with the side-drum, for marching and for dancing; a very few pictures show flutes being played in what would now be called chamber music.

According to Praetorius, in the first great musical encyclopaedia (1619), the *Schweizerpfeiff*, or fife, was narrower in bore, with a shriller sound, than the *Querpfeiff*, or transverse flute, and was tuned and fingered slightly differently. He gives three sizes for the cross flutes, saying that their lowest notes are A for the canto, D for the tenor, and G for the bass. The tenor became the normal concert flute of the baroque period and remains so today; the bass is the present-day alto flute.

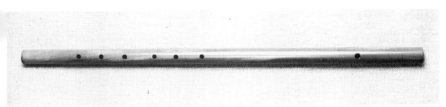

Copy by Lewis Jones of one of the renaissance flutes in the Accademia Filarmonica of Verona. (Bate Collection 1107.)

BAROQUE FLUTES

Around the 1670s the flute's design was radically altered by makers at the French court at Versailles, who developed new constructional techniques. A cylindrical flute cannot be in tune; some conicity is essential to get the overblown notes of the upper register into tune with the lower. They designed a cylindrical headjoint and a conical body, widest at the head end, narrowing towards the foot. Fingerholes affect the tuning; each forms a small chamber in the bore, a short chimney through the wood. The flutemaker's skill lies in making very small adjustments to the bore to compensate for these chambers; by separating the head from the body, it became easier to make these adjustments.

The first baroque flutes, for which composers such as Couperin wrote much chamber music, were made in three joints: the head, with the embouchure drilled in it, the body with the six fingerholes, and a new foot with an extra hole, covered by a key. The foot was needed because music was becoming more complex and elaborate. Opening the holes of a baroque flute in sequence, one produces a diatonic scale of D major: D with all holes covered, E with the first

Copy by Felix Raudonikas, Leningrad, of the flute by Hotteterre in the Leningrad Music Instrument Museum, one of the only three to survive; in three joints (head, body and foot); made in rosewood and mammoth ivory since the materials of the original, boxwood and elephant ivory were unavailable. (Bate Collection x1047.)

hole open, F sharp with the next, G with the third, and so on. One plays in other keys by cross-fingering, opening one hole and closing others below it, thus flattening the pitch. However, there are no holes available for closing below the lowest hole; instead, the key-covered hole was opened for the lowest chromatic note. Keys are named from the note produced by their operation, so this first key was called the D sharp or E flat key.

The new flute quickly gained popularity with the more progressive musicians. It was capable of far greater expressiveness and sensibility than the recorder, which had been regarded as a much more respectable instrument and indeed was still called *the* flute until after the middle of the eighteenth century. The transverse flute was specified either by that name or as the 'German flute'; 'flute', by itself, meant recorder. But now the musician who fancied a flute was likely to take to the German flute, and the most famous player who did so was Frederick the Great of Prussia. Through the influence of such patrons, and the desire for expressiveness, the *traversa* or transverse flute gained ascendancy over the recorder. Frederick the Great wrote many concertos and other solos himself, but better

known is the work which Bach wrote to impress him, the 'Trio Sonata' in *The Musical Offering*. Bach wrote a number of other works for the transverse flute, probably the best known being the *Suite no. 2 in B minor*.

The recorder is less expressive because it cannot, except within narrow limits, play softer or louder. When blown louder, the pitch gets sharper; as one blows more softly, the pitch goes flat, and there is very little the player can do to compensate. The *traversa* behaves exactly the same, but players can counteract such pitch changes. By rolling the embouchure inwards so that the lip covers it slightly, its area is reduced and the pitch flattened; rolling it outwards, opening it slightly, sharpens the pitch. Thus, to produce louder sounds, the player blows harder, sharpening the pitch, simultaneously rolling the flute towards his mouth, flattening the pitch by the same amount and therefore staying in tune. The description is complicated, but doing it becomes instinctive with practice.

In the second quarter of the eighteenth century the flute changed again. Just as the earlier makers found it advantageous to make the flute in three joints, the next

One-key flute in four joints (head, upper body, lower body and foot) by Charles Bizey, Paris, early eighteenth century; boxwood with ivory mounts. (Bate Collection 106.)

Katharine Bircher playing an ivory flute by Thomas Stanesby junior, London, c.1735. (Bate Collection x1050.)

generation found it even better to use four. The body joint was divided, with three fingerholes in each half. This had three main advantages: economy of wood, because shorter billets could be used; greater accuracy in reaming the bore; and, above all, greater ease in tuning to other instruments.

There was then no standard pitch and most towns had their own pitch, or even pitches, for the organs in each church might be tuned differently, these might differ from the opera house, and all might differ from the pitch used for chamber music. Although one could pull the tenons of the joints a little out of their sockets to lengthen the tube and flatten the pitch, this leaves a cavity in the bore between the end of the tenon and the bottom of the socket. Such cavities play havoc with the tuning. The solution was the *corps de rechange*, a set of upper body joints, each a slightly different length; players could use whichever put the instrument in tune. Johann Joachim Quantz, Frederick the Great's flute teacher, court composer, and author of the most famous book on playing the flute, also recommended the use of *corps de rechange* for music which was particularly loud or soft. A shorter joint to sharpen the pitch compensates for gentler blowing which would otherwise

flatten it, and a longer joint would prevent louder music from being sharp.

Another of Quantz's recommendations was a second key. While D sharp

One-key ivory flute by John Just Schuchart, London, in its original case; mid eighteenth century; with the three corps de rechange which survive from the original set of six. (Bate Collection 101.)

7

Above: *Foot joint of an ebony flute by Friedrich Gabriel August Kirst, Potsdam; late eighteenth century; showing the separate keys for E flat and D sharp as recommended by Quantz. (Bate Collection 118.)*

and E flat are the same note in the equal temperament we use today, in the eighteenth century's meantone temperament E flat is nearly a quartertone higher than D sharp. Meantone was a tuning system in which most of the thirds were exactly in tune (in our equal temperament they are very sharp), but as a result some of the fifths and fourths were less well tuned. Also as a result, all the enharmonics, the sharps and flats, which on a keyboard must share one key, were really each two quite different notes. D sharp, a major third above B, was lower than E flat, a minor third above C. Quantz's flutes, and Frederick the Great's, therefore had two keys, the holes under them differing slightly in diameter, one for E flat and the other for D sharp.

(Left to right) Four-key rosewood flute by Cahusac, late eighteenth century, with keys for D sharp/ E flat, F natural, G sharp/A flat, and B flat; five-key boxwood flute by William Milhouse, early nineteenth century (four-key plus upper C natural); six-key boxwood flute by Milhouse (four-key with C-foot); eight-key ivory flute by Tebaldo Monzani, 1818 (six-key plus long F natural and upper C natural). All made in London. (Bate Collection 111, x1081, 121, and x17.)

Body and foot joints of a boxwood seven-key flute by Tebaldo Monzani, London, c.1815; with keys for middle C and C sharp, D sharp/E flat, F natural, G sharp/A flat, B flat, and upper C natural. (Bate Collection x16.)

THE CLASSICAL PERIOD OF MOZART AND HAYDN

Keys are sprung either to stand closed, to be opened by the finger, or held open, to be closed by the finger. The E flat or D sharp key was closed-standing. In the 1760s the range was extended downwards by a longer foot joint carrying two open-standing keys which, when closed, produced C sharp and middle C.

At much the same date new closed-standing keys replaced the cross-fingerings for F natural, G sharp or A flat, B flat and the upper C natural. These keys were needed because, whereas musicians of the baroque period enjoyed the veiled sound of cross-fingered chromatic notes, this was less admired by the next generation and their successors such as Mozart and Haydn. Composers were now writing in new keys, and flautists, like everyone else, were expected to play in almost any key. Notes foreign to D major were required more often and had to sound the same as the other notes.

Hence were developed the four-key flute, with the E flat or D sharp key and the F natural key for the right hand and the G sharp or A flat key and the B flat key for the left hand, and the six-key flute, the same plus the extension to middle C. A second F natural, a long key allowing the left little finger to play that commonest of accidentals, instead of the right ring-finger, and the upper C nat-ural, a longer key for the right forefinger, were added. These established the eight-key flute, the standard instrument of the first half of the nineteenth century, still a popular instrument in Ireland and in flute bands.

The brass or silver keys were mounted in wooden blocks. A narrow channel through the block took the shank of the key, with an axle running through shank and block. A brass strip, hammer-hardened as a spring, was riveted to the touch piece of the key, its other end resting on the floor of the channel to keep the key closed. A flat pad of kid leather, stuck to the underside of the key-head with shellac or sealing wax, covered the hole. The two open-standing keys were made in two pieces, each with its own axle, with the spring under the touch. The touch was held upwards by the spring, and when pressed down its other end rose, pushing up the nearer end of the second piece to bring the key-head down and close its hole.

Kid pads on open-standing keys tended to leak. The constant pressure of a closed key's pad on its hole beds it down, just as the shape of a hole appears on one's finger after pressing on it. Because they stood open, the extension keys never bedded down properly, and a leaking key ruins the tone quality and prevents notes from sounding. In 1785

9

Left: *Detail of a D sharp/E flat key, inverted to show the spring and the kid-leather pad.*

Right: *Detail of the channel for the D sharp/ E flat key cut in the wooden socket bulge of the foot joint.*

Left: *Detail of the open-standing foot keys of a flute by William Henry Potter, London, c.1815, showing the pewter plugs used instead of pads. (Bate Collection 1060.)*

Right: *The foot joint of a Potter flute without the keys, showing the brass bushing and the channels through the blocks.*

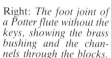

Richard Potter patented pewter plugs for all his keys, which many makers used for most of the next century on the open-standing keys. The holes were lined with brass, to provide a hard edge, and the cone-shaped plugs of soft pewter bedded down firmly on the brass, eliminating all risk of leakage.

In the same patent Potter described the screw cork and tuning slide. The exact position of the cork above the

embouchure is critical for tuning. When altering the length of the flute to tune it, the distance between embouchure and cork should also slightly alter. The end cap was usually of ivory, and an ivory screw with a threaded shank passed through its centre; the other end screwed into the cork. As the cap was turned, the screw was either drawn out, which drew out the cork, or pushed in. A fifth joint, the barrel, had a socket for the tenon of

10

e upper body joint at one end and a ining slide at the other. The slide was ngraved with lines, and when drawn to, or instance, the second line, the head ap was turned so the screw also showed ne second line. The tuning slide, which eplaced the *corps de rechange*, consisted of two thin brass tubes, sliding telecopically with no gap or chamber in the ore.

These late eighteenth-century flutes, or which Mozart, Haydn and Beethoven wrote, sounded very different from the modern flute. They were quieter, because of the conical bore and small fingerholes, and sweeter, because boxwood, of which they were made, produces a very sweet and mellow sound. They differed also from the flute used by Bach and Handel, for they were brighter and louder because the keys replaced cross-fingering and the embouchure was larger. These differences are appreciated today, and one can often hear music of these periods, such as Mozart's flute quartets, played on the instruments for which it was written. Only in this way can we understand the intentions of earlier composers when they wrote their music.

Above: *The ivory cap, ivory screw and cork removed from a flute.*

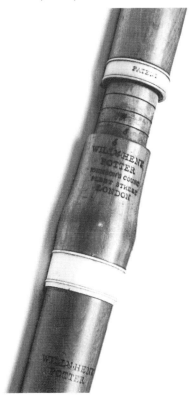

Right: *The tuning barrel of a flute by William Henry Potter, c.1815, showing the marked lines and the tuning slide.*

Below: *Six-key boxwood flute by William Henry Potter, London, c.1815, with all pewter plugs, screw cork and tuning barrel. See opposite and above for details of the foot keys and tuning barrel. (Bate Collection 1060.)*

Above: *Four-key glass flute ('crystale' in French), by either Claude Laurent or J. D. Breton, Paris; first half of the nineteenth century. (Bate Collection 120.)* Top: *Detail of a key on the flute, mounted between pillars on a bed-plate.*

NEW MATERIALS FOR FLUTES

From the beginning of the nineteenth century changes came rapidly. Some were due to the growth of technology and others to the increase of trade with South America, Africa and the East. New woods became available, harder, denser and more stable than boxwood, such as rosewood, grenadilla, cocus and ebony.

Claude Laurent of Paris patented glass flutes in 1806. Glass is more stable than any wood, but difficult to work in the lathe, which made the traditional methods of mounting the keys impracticable. Laurent soldered pairs of short metal pillars to bed-plates, attaching these to the surface of the flute, with each key on an axle between the pillars;

he was the first to use pillars consistently. The shape and material of the keys changed. Instead of a narrow waist to lie in the channel between the blocks, keys mounted between pillars have trunnions, drilled to take the axle, projecting from the waist to reach from one pillar to the other. The white bronzes (such as German silver), invented about 1830, were stronger than brass and cheaper than real silver.

Early in the nineteenth century the clarinetist Iwan Müller introduced new materials for pads. His thin kid-leather wool-stuffed purse was more springy than the flat pad and sealed the holes more effectively. However, such pads could not be securely fixed to flat keys,

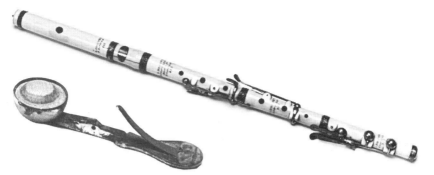

Eight-key ivory flute by Louis Drouët, London, c.1820; with silver cup-keys for the new stuffed pads. Because Drouët's flutes were frequently forged, it has a silver guarantee plaque on the barrel to certify that it is a genuine Drouët flute. (Bate Collection x14.) Insert: Detail of a cup-key, inverted to show the pad.

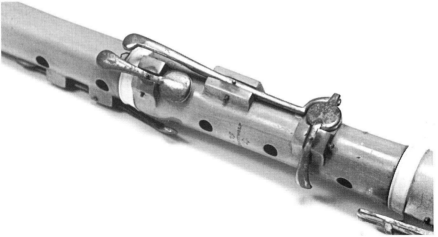

Boxwood flute by Johann Heinrich Gottlieb Streitwolf, Göttingen, early nineteenth century. The long F lever hooks under a projection on the head of the cross F natural key and lifts it from that end. (Bate Collection 1026.)

Detail of the two F natural keys of the Streitwolf flute. The use of this 'Tromlitz lever' avoids boring a second F natural hole.

13

and so a new cupped key-head was devised into which they could be glued. Johann Georg Tromlitz suggested the use of double levers in 1800. Instead of two keys covering two alternative holes, a single hole could be covered by a key operated both by the usual touch piece and by a lever which, hooking under the key-head, would lift it from that end. This reduced the number of cavities in the bore and improved the tuning. Tromlitz levers were used by many makers, among them Tebaldo Monzani of London.

Monzani improved the sockets and tenons which link the joints. The traditional wooden tenon, lapped with waxed thread, fitted into a wooden socket which, to withstand pushing the tenon into it, was supported by a bulge in the wood and usually a ferrule of ivory or other material. Monzani replaced the thread by a thin layer of cork on a silver sleeve and lined the socket internally with silver, which gave enough support without the wooden bulge.

The flute's material was also affected by the desire to reduce cost. Wood must be seasoned before it becomes stable enough to be used. When seasoned, it is sawn and turned on the lathe, and it may then reveal flaws, becoming valueless. This is one reason why ebonite or vulcanite, specially processed rubber, was welcomed by woodwind makers when introduced about 1840. In addition, it retained its dimensions better than wood, was easy and cheap to work and was popular for use in areas with extremes of humidity and temperature, because it is unaffected by atmospheric changes.

Ebonite was praised for its tone

Rosewood flute by Tebaldo Monzani, London, 1812; with Tromlitz levers to the F natural and B flat keys. Monzani was one of the few makers to have the silver keys hallmarked; thus many of his flutes can be dated precisely. (Bate Collection 1065.)

Detail of wooden socket and silver socket, both by Monzani. (Bate Collection x16 and 126.)

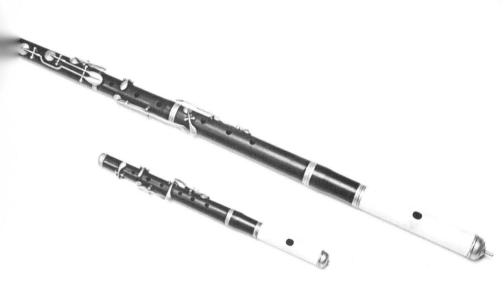

Eight-key blackwood flute with ivory head, and a matching piccolo; both anonymous German, late nineteenth century. (Bate Collection x104 and x115.)

quality, though today it is more often used by beginners and schoolchildren than by professional musicians. The question of whether materials influence sound is continually debated by acousticians and players. Most acousticians maintain that tone is controlled by the air column and that the material which encloses it has no influence. Most players are certain that flutes of different materials produce different sounds, even though their internal shapes are identical.

Before 1950 almost all British players used wooden flutes, but then the French silver flute became more popular, and now the wooden flute is very rarely heard. Even silver fails to satisfy some, and gold or, for those who could not afford all gold, a gold head and a silver body are often seen today. Players say that the material of the head has more influence than that of the body, which is why the gold head is often used, just as in Germany an ivory head was often used

with a wooden body. Gold is used because the denser the material the stronger the sound. Some have therefore tried platinum, which is denser than gold, but the weight and the cost are greater, and the sound little better.

Silver is expensive, so various alloys and silver-plated brass are also used. Now that the rain-forests where hardwoods grow are dwindling as fast as the demand for instruments is increasing, it is perhaps as well that the sound of metal flutes is preferred. Metal also has considerable advantages for mass production. Until the mid nineteenth century most makers were individual craftsmen with a few helpers and apprentices. Larger firms came into being and factories were set up to produce instruments in considerable numbers. The modern explosion of demand has resulted in automated assembly lines producing instruments like any other commodity, and this is only possible with metal or plastic instruments.

Right: *Portrait of Charles Nicholson (1795-1837) by T. Cart, 1834. Nicholson is holding one of his own wide-hole model flutes, made of cocus wood with silver mounts, probably made by Thomas Prowse. His left hand obscures the characteristic hollow in the upper joint, which was another of his developments to make the flute easier to hold. (National Portrait Gallery.)*

Below: *Eight-key 'Nicholson's Improved' cocus flute, sold by Clementi and Company, London, probably made by Thomas Prowse, c.1822. (Bate Collection x1048.)*

Bottom: *Detail of the large fingerholes of the Nicholson flute.*

Detail of the clutch on a Boehm system flute.

THE DEVELOPMENT OF THE MODERN FLUTE

Popular desire to 'listen to music grew with changes in society in the late eighteenth and early nineteenth centuries. Over much of Europe, concerts had usually been given before small audiences in the salons of the aristocracy. Public concerts, whose costs must be covered by those who come to hear them, demand large concert halls, and then musicians have to make more sound to be heard. Thus orchestras grew larger and instruments grew louder.

The first player to change the flute to make it louder was Charles Nicholson. In 1822 he greatly increased the fingerhole diameters, venting their sound more clearly. His large-hole flute became popular with some players, though others thought it too loud. Flutes on his model were made throughout the nineteenth century.

Nicholson's flute had a far-reaching effect on a young German flautist and goldsmith, Theobald Boehm, when he visited London. Determined to make an equally loud, clear sound, Boehm experimented with flute designs, producing one model in 1831 in London and another on his return to Munich in 1832. These still had conical bodies, with somewhat larger fingerholes than Nicholson's, but differently arranged, with new keywork to control them. The 1832 Boehm flute, or conical Boehm, was immediately recognised as a considerable improvement by many players and was produced in Germany, France and Britain under licence.

The main French maker, Auguste Buffet, introduced several refinements, the most important of which were the clutch, by which a key can transmit

1832 system boxwood flute by Theobald Boehm, Munich, c.1840, the so-called Conical Boehm. (Bate Collection 166.)

motion to another key, and the needle spring. Instead of mounting the keys individually, Boehm used long rod axles, mounting rings and keys on sleeves which permitted them to move independently of the axle; the clutch allowed the sleeve, and the key, to be moved by the axle. Thus a key could be moved without disturbing other keys, but it could be moved, by the clutch, by moving another key on the same axle. These long axles had two further results. One was that the two body joints were reunited so that axles could run the whole length. The other was that boxwood was abandoned because, as the London maker Cornelius Ward said, boxwood was more suited to a hygrometer than a musical instrument — it expanded and contracted so much with changes in humidity that the axles and clutches either jammed or failed to articulate.

After fifteen years working in the Bavarian steel industry, Boehm returned to the flute and completely redesigned it. He changed to a cylindrical bore, avoiding the resulting tuning difficulties by introducing a parabolic head-joint, tapering towards the embouchure. He calculated acoustically ideal sizes and positions for fingerholes, with the result that they were too wide for the fingers to cover and too far apart for the span of the hand. All had therefore to be covered by

Conical Boehm cocus flute by Clair Godefroy senior, Paris, one of Boehm's licensed makers: mid nineteenth century. (Bate Collection 155.)

Body of a cocus cylindrical Boehm system flute by Rudall, Carte and Company, London; stripped of all its keywork so that the sizes and positions of the holes may be seen. (Bate Collection 161.)

1847 system silver flute by Theobald Boehm, Munich, c.1850, the so-called Cylindrical Boehm. (Bate Collection 150.)

Siccama patent conical cocus flute. The holes for the ring-finger of each hand are nearer their correct acoustical positions and beyond the reach of the finger; they are therefore covered by a key which is a third-order lever. (Bate Collection 162.)

Katharine Bircher playing a cocus-wood Siccama system flute. (Bate Collection 162.)

keys, for which he designed a new mechanism. The 1847 system, the cylindrical Boehm, was a great advance over the 1832 flute and is, in all essentials and with only minor changes, the instrument used today.

One of the main changes is to the G sharp key. While a closed-standing key needs a powerful spring to hold it closed, an open-standing key needs only a weak spring to hold it open and to reopen it. A player must overcome the pressure of the springs, whichever way the keys are set, and obviously it is easier to work against weak springing than powerful; Boehm therefore sprung them all open. However, the majority of players preferred a closed G sharp, so many makers produced Boehm system flutes with Dorus's modification for that key. Boehm himself made a few flutes with a closed G sharp, using a special design of his own.

Some players rejected the 1847 system because it involved new fingering patterns. Musicians practice for many hours until their fingers acquire automatic responses; there is seldom time to think how a note should be fingered — the fingers must fall immediately into the right positions. Such automatic responses are very difficult to alter. However, it was undeniable that the 1847 flute sounded vastly better than the old eight-key instrument, and so makers attempted to produce compromise instruments which would sound as good as the Boehm but which could be fingered like the eight-key.

Abel Siccama's Diatonic Flute was one, but as it was still a conical flute, with Nicholson fingerholes, two of which, by using third-order levers, were nearer their proper positions, its success was not lasting. Four years later, Richard Carte brought out a far better compromise, his 1851 system. This looked and sounded like a Boehm, having a cylindrical body with parabolic head and all the holes covered by keys, but was fingered basically like an eight-key flute. Others, such as Rockstro and Clinton, produced models on a conical body, both with

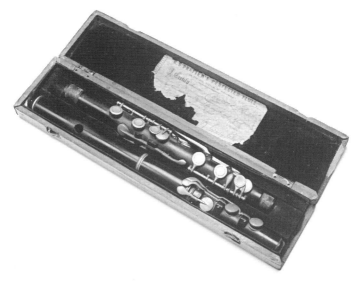

Conical Pratten's Perfected Flute by Boosey and Sons, London, c.1860; with its original case with Pratten's certificate pasted into the lid. (Bate Collection x110.)

1851 system silver flute by Rudall, Rose, Carte and Company, London, post 1862; Carte's system with Boehm's parabola and cylindrical bore. (Bate Collection x1057.)

Conical cocus flute by Cornelius Ward, London, c.1840, with the cross-over keys of his first system. One of the many British rivals to the Boehm system. (Bate Collection 163.)

Conical cocus flute by Clinton and Company, London, c.1865; John Clinton's Equisonant Flute. (Bate Collection 153.)

Rockstro's system cocus flute by Rudall, Carte and Company, London, 1873. A variant of the cylindrical Boehm. (Bate Collection x128.)

some initial success, but Clinton eventually changed to a cylindrical body and Rockstro to his own version of Boehm's system. Sidney Pratten also produced a new conical flute, calling it Pratten's Perfected. He then changed to a cylindrical body, devising a number of different systems, all based on the eight-key and all called Pratten's Perfected. The most important English design was Carte's 1867 system, slightly different from Boehm's design but, in the opinion of many players, an improvement of it, which was used more often than the Boehm in Britain until the 1930s.

Elsewhere, it was mainly in Germany that resistance to Boehm's design was encountered. The Reform Flute was conical, with an elaboration of the eight-key fingering, using Tromlitz levers and several vent and trill keys. Another feature of the German and eastern European flute is the extension by a further semitone, to the low B. This extension also proved popular in the United States of America, for the Boehm flute, which is universally used there, can be extended as easily as the Reform. Most players in Britain and France, however, still use flutes which descend only to C.

Development has not ceased with the almost universal adoption of the Boehm system today. A number of players have developed new systems or further improvements, and such progress is inevitable with all instruments. There is continual change in the conditions of music-making, and in the music itself, and these changes are reflected in, or sometimes induced by, changes in the instruments that play the music.

Radcliffe system cylindrical cocus flute by Rudall, Carte and Company, London, 1889. A simplified version of the 1851 system, for which see opposite. (Bate Collection x107.)

Schwedler and Kruspe's Reform flute by Carl Kruspe, Leipzig, c.1900; blackwood with extension to low B natural. (Bate Collection 1102.)

Martin system silver flute by Rudall, Carte and Company, London, post 1878; a complex version of the Radcliffe system. (Bate Collection x109.)

1867 system silver flute by Rudall, Carte and Company, London, post 1878; the most successful variant of the cylindrical Boehm. (Bate Collection 160.)

Boehm system flute to low B natural by F. Barbier, Paris, c.1875; square-section silver tube with *later* Louis Lot head of normal shape. (Bate Collection 1032.)

Boehm system silver flute to low B flat by Eugène Albert, Brussels, second half of the nineteenth century. (Bate Collection 1090.)

James Mathews's 'Chrysostom' by Rudall, Rose, Carte and Company, London, 1868; the most complex of all the elaborations of the 1851 system. (Bate Collection 1039.)

Alexander Murray system flute, the most promising of the modern post-Boehm systems. (Bate Collection 1101.)

23

Piccolos: (from top to bottom) one-key ivory by Whitaker, London, 1823; four-key boxwood by Hérouard Frères, Paris, mid-nineteenth century; six-key cocus by Hays, London, c.1883; Boehm system cocus by Godefroy, Paris, pre-1878. (Bate Collection 187, 193, x116 and 175.)

OTHER SIZES OF FLUTE

The commonest of the other sizes of flute is the piccolo, a small instrument sounding an octave higher. It came into orchestral use around 1800; the piccolo parts written by Vivaldi were probably for a small flageolet, a whistle flute like a simple recorder. Rameau's piccolo parts, however, were probably written for a transverse piccolo with one key. Few piccolos were extended to C sharp and C, but otherwise their fingering parallels that of the flute.

Larger flutes have always existed but have only been commonly used in flute bands and, since the 1960s or so, in recording studios. Their sound, particularly in the lower register, is easily covered by other instruments and lost, but in studios, where instruments each have their own microphone, they can be boosted for balance. Orchestrally they

have been mainly used by French composers, notably Debussy and Ravel, who have written for them with the necessary care in much of their orchestral music. There are three sizes. The true bass, an octave lower than the ordinary instrument, is rarely seen. The alto, whose lowest note is G, is the instrument Debussy and Ravel wrote for. Alto and bass flutes have the same fingering system as the normal instrument, but they both have the 'C foot' which, on the alto, provides G sharp and G and, on the true bass, low C sharp and C. Much rarer is the *flûte d'amour*, a tone higher than the alto. This is sometimes confused with ordinary flutes with long extensions to A, instead of the normal C or B. The extended flute achieves its lowest note with extra foot keys, whereas the *flûte d'amour* produces it by closing its six fin-

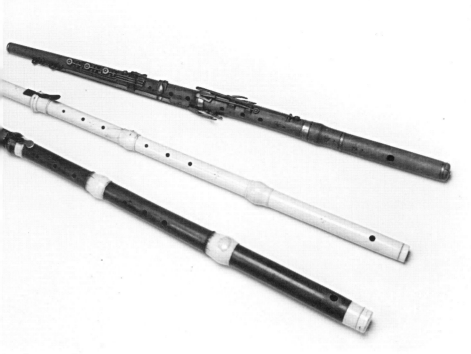

...ûtes d'amour in boxwood by Thomas Stanesby junior, London, c.1735, and in ivory by Scherer, ...tzbach mid-eighteenth century, with a boxwood flute to low A by Luvoni, Milan, late nineteenth ...ntury. While the total lengths are similar, the positions of the six fingerholes show that the flûtes ...mour are low-pitched instruments, whereas the Luvoni is an ordinary flute with an extended foot. ...ate Collection 1015, 1011 and x105.)

...xwood band flutes: (from top to bottom) fife, anonymous, eighteenth century; B flat flute by ...ristopher Gerock, London, early nineteenth century; F flute by Richard Potter, London, late ...hteenth century. (Bate Collection 188, 174 and 1004.)

Katharine Bircher playing a metal double-tube flute extended to low A by Agostino Rampone, Milan, late nineteenth century. (Bate Collection x19.)

gerholes. While there seems to be littl**e** repertoire for the *flûte d'amour*, it **is** thought that it was often used to pla**y** normal flute music, such as Bach's so**n**atas, transposed to a lower pitch, for th**e** sake of its beautifully rich tone quality**.**

Other sizes are band instrument**s.** These have been distinct from th**e** orchestral instruments since the re**naissance.** They are named in Brita**in** from the note produced by closing s**ix** fingerholes, and the resulting pitch, an**d** thus the name, varies according to the**ir** size.

The normal soprano is the fife or B fl**at** flute; the fifes and drums were for ce**n**turies the standard military band an**d** were taken on campaign and, with th**e** bugle, used in the field. Fife bands r**e**main popular in many parts of Brita**in** and especially in Ireland, where the**y** outnumber brass and military band**s.** Above the B flat flute are various sizes **of** piccolo, usually in E flat and F. Belo**w** the B flat come the F flute, the bass in **B** flat, and the contrabass in F and E fla**t,** usually with a U-shaped head-joint **to** make the instrument more portabl**e.** Many bands keep to simple system ke**y**work, either the six closed keys of th**e** eight-key flute without the C extensio**n** or with various of Pratten's perfection**s** on conical or cylindrical bodies. Some **of** the more advanced bands use the Ra**d**cliffe or the Carte Guards model, bas**ed** on the 1867 system, and a few use th**e** normal Boehm system.

*Cocus B flat bass flute by Rudall and Rose, London, c.1825, and metal F contrabass flute w**ith** curled head-joint by Rudall, Carte and Company, London, twentieth century. (Bate Collection 10**11** and 1012.)*

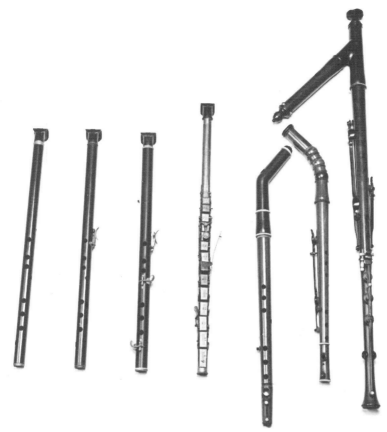

Eccentric flutes. (Left to right) Giorgi patent keyless; Giorgi patent with one key; Giorgi patent with three keys (all by Joseph Wallis and Son, London, 1896 and after); Schaffner system flute by Giorgi, Florence, c.1888; one-key, three-key, and alto flutes, all in mahogany, all devised by Dr Burghley of Camden Town, London, second half of nineteenth century. (Bate Collection 1020, 1021, 1068, 1019, 1016-18.)

ECCENTRIC FLUTES

Some nineteenth-century flute-makers were adamantly opposed to Boehm and all his works. They believed that the proliferation of keys was the ruination of the flute. Dr Burghley of Camden Town in London was one of the first of these. He was also conscious of the muscular effort of holding the flute in the normal position, which often leads to neck strain. He devised his flutes with the minimum number of keys, on the old conical bore pattern, and with bent or angled head-joints so that his flutes could be held in a less physically awkward position. Very little is known of him, not even who made his flutes for him, or whether he made them himself.

Signor Giorgi of Florence went further. He abolished keys altogether but retained Boehm's cylindrical bore and was determined also to retain Boehm's principle of a hole for each note of the chromatic scale. There are twelve notes in the chromatic scale. One of these is

Left: *Katharine Bircher playing the mahogany alto (bass) flute by Dr Burghley of Camden Town. (Bate Collection 1018.)*

Right: *Boehm system bass flute to low B natural; Albisiphone, by Abelardo Albisi, Milan, c.1910. The true bass flute is so long and heavy that Albisi considered it easier to hold it vertically than horizontally. (Bate Collection 1022.)*

ovided by the open end of the flute, but this still leaves eleven to be controlled by ten fingers, which also have to support the instrument. Both thumbs and all the fingers have a hole each, the eleventh hole being covered by the side of the left forefinger, whose tip is already covering another hole. To play such a flute transversely would be almost impossible, so he placed the embouchure at T-head at the top of the flute. His instruments were surprisingly popular and were made in ebonite and sold in large numbers by Joseph Wallis and Son. However, the eleventh hole caused such problems that eventually a key was provided to help the left forefinger cover it, and before long several more keys were added, thus essentially defeating the whole purpose of his design.

The most successful flute played in this way is Abelardo Albisi's Albisiphone, a bass flute of very wide bore, which would be far too heavy to hold out sideways.

This has a head very similar to Giorgi's flutes, but more sensibly has full Boehm system keywork and a ring to take the hook of a neck strap like that of a saxophone.

Little or nothing is known of Giorgi's other pattern of flute, which combines Giorgi's T-head and Boehm's cylindrical bore with an extremely elaborate key system devised by a Florentine dentist named Schaffner. This has rectangular holes, graduated in size, covered with rectangular plates, each of which has engraved upon it the musical depiction of the note to which it applies. These are controlled by a complex system of tracker rods which require very delicate adjustment. It is curious that the patent for this system is eight years earlier than that for the keyless flute, and that in none of the publicity which Giorgi issued for the keyless instrument is there any mention of the Schaffner system.

RECENT DEVELOPMENTS

There have been two major developments in the second half of the twentieth century, one to the flute, the other to its playing. The former is the electric flute, whose cork is often replaced by a microphone. The sound can be fed into an amplifier, passed through filters, band passes, fuzz boxes and all the other gadgets of modern electronics, and the sound manipulated in any way that players, composers or sound-engineers desire.

The other important development is the production of new sounds with non-standard fingerings. Discovered initially by accident and then by players experimenting with fingerings, these have been exploited by a number of composers, of whom the best known are probably Berio and Ligeti. They were first described in print by Bruno Bartolozzi, who lists fingerings and different lip formations to produce quartertones and other small intervals, trills with a single fingering, rolling or widely vibrated notes, and multi-note chords. Exploring these possibilities and mastering them sufficiently for performance requires considerable skill and practice, but anyone with access to a Boehm system flute, and the ability to read a simple fingering chart, can produce many of these effects.

REPERTOIRE FOR THE FLUTE

Much music was written in the baroque period for 'flute or violin', 'flute or oboe', and similar vague phrases. While this list is restricted to works specifically for the flute, Mozart's *Flute Concerto*, K.314, which is in fact an oboe concerto adapted to the flute, is included. Much other music may be heard on record, radio and in the concert hall which is not listed here. Many composers wrote so much for the flute that it would be invidious to make a selection of their work. Thus only their names and an indication of the sort of music they wrote are listed here. Even more was arranged for one or two flutes, for example *Favourite Airs from Messiah* (and the 'Hallelujah Chorus' for two flutes and bass), selections from most of Mozart's operas, many Haydn symphonies, and so forth.

FOR RENAISSANCE KEYLESS FLUTE
Morley, T.: *Consort Lessons*. 1599.
Also much dance music published by Attaignant, Praetorius and others can be played very effectively on a quartet of renaissance transverse flutes of different sizes.

FOR EARLY BAROQUE FLUTE
(These were the composers and musicians of the French court)
Couperin, F.: trio sonatas.
Hotteterre, J. M.: sonatas and suites.
La Barre, M. de: suites.
Marais, M.: suites.

FOR LATER BAROQUE FLUTE
(and possibly the earlier type also)
Bach, C. P. E.: much music written for his employer, Frederick the Great.
Bach, J. S.: *Brandenburg Concerto no. 5*, BWV 1050.
Bach, J. S.: *Sonatas* including the Trio Sonata from *The Musical Offering*, BWV 1079 no. 8.
Bach, J. S.: *Suite no. 2 in B minor* for flute and strings, BWV 1067.
Boismortier, J. B. de: trio sonatas.
Frederick the Great: some 600 or more works for the flute, much of it of good quality.

Handel, G. F.: sonatas.
Loeillet, John: trio sonatas.
Quantz, J. J.: much music written for his employer, Frederick the Great.
Stanley, J.: solos (i.e. sonatas).
Telemann, G. P.: sonatas and other chamber music.
Vivaldi, A.: concertos.

FOR LATER ONE-KEY FLUTE
Bach, J. C.: concertos and a good deal of chamber music.
Devienne, F. J.: innumerable concertos and chamber music.
LeClair, J. M.: concertos and sonatas.
Stamitz, J. W. A.: concertos.

FOR FOUR TO EIGHT-KEY FLUTE
Beethoven, L. van: *Serenade* op.25.
Boccherini, L.: concertos, sonatas, and chamber music.
Cambini, G. G.: concertos and chamber music.
Corrette, M.: concertos, sonatas, etc.
Dussek, J. L.: sonatas.
Gluck, C. W. 'Danse of the Blessed Spirits' in *Orphée et Eurydice*, Wotquenne 30.
Haydn, F. J.: some sonatas and chamber music.
Hoffmeister, F. A.: 30 concertos and much chamber music.
Köhler, G. H.: many sonatas, etc.
Krommer, F.: concertos and chamber music.
Mozart, W. A.: *Concerto for flute*, K.313 (285c).
Mozart, W. A.: *Concerto for flute*, (originally oboe), K.314 (285d).
Mozart, W. A.: *Concerto for flute and harp*, K.299 (297c).
Mozart, W. A.: *Andante for flute*, K.315 (285e).
Mozart, W. A.: *Quartets* for flute and strings, K.285, 298, and K.Anh.171 (285b).
Rosetti, F. A.: concertos.
Sammartini, G. B.: concertos and chamber music.
Stamitz, A.: concertos.
Stamitz, C. P.: concertos and chamber music.
Vanhal, J. B.: concertos, sonatas, etc.

OR BOEHM SYSTEM FLUTE

erkeley, L.: *Concerto*, op.36.
erlioz, H.: 'The Flight into Egypt' in
   L'Enfance du Christ, Holoman 130.
haminade, C.: *Concertino*, op.107.
ebussy, C.: *Syrinx* for solo flute.
ebussy, C.: *Prélude à L'Après-Midi
   d'un Faune*.
lenze, H. W.: *Sonatina*.
lindemith, P.: *Sonata*.
bert, J.: *Concerto*.
bert, J.: *Sonatine*.
acob, G.: *Concerto*.
lielsen, C.: *Concerto*, op.119.
oulenc, F.: *Sonata*.
rokofiev, S.: *Sonata*, op.94.
aint-Saëns, C.: 'Volière' in *Carnival of
   the Animals*.

Since the flute has been the top voice in the orchestra since the latter part of the eighteenth century, and thus more audible than most other woodwind, it seems unnecessary to cite orchestral works in which it features other than the four particularly well known solos by Gluck, Berlioz, Debussy and Saint-Saëns which are listed above.

Save for performances on 'authentic' instruments, all this repertoire is normally played today on the metal Boehm flute and therefore will not sound as most of the composers listed here originally intended it.

FURTHER READING

Baines, Anthony. *Woodwind Instruments and their History*. Faber and Faber, third edition 1967.

Bartolozzi, Bruno. *New Sounds for Woodwind*. Oxford University Press, second edition 1982.

Bate, Philip. *The Flute*. Ernest Benn, 1969.

Benade, Arthur. *Fundamentals of Musical Acoustics*. Oxford University Press, 1976.

Boehm, Theobald. *The Flute and Flute-Playing* (translated by Dayton Miller). Dover, New York, 1964.

Hotteterre, Jacques. *Principes de la Flute Traversiere*. Amsterdam, 1728. (Facsimile, Bärenreiter, Kassel, 1958; translation by David Lasocki, Barrie and Jenkins, 1968.)

Montagu, Jeremy. *The World of Medieval and Renaissance Musical Instruments*. David and Charles, 1976.

Montagu, Jeremy. *The World of Baroque and Classical Musical Instruments*. David and Charles, 1979.

Montagu, Jeremy. *The World of Romantic and Modern Musical Instruments*. David and Charles, 1981.

Praetorius, Michael. *Syntagma Musicum,* volume II, *De Organographia*. Wolffenbüttel, 1619. (Facsimile, Bärenreiter, Kassel, 1968; translation by David Crookes, Oxford University Press, 1986.)

Quantz, Johann Joachim. *Versuch einer Anweisung die Flöte traversiere zu spielen*. Berlin, 1752. (Facsimile, Bärenreiter, Kassel, 1953; translation by Edward Reilly, Faber, 1966.)

Rockstro, Richard Shepherd. *A Treatise on . . . The Flute*. Rudall Carte, 1889. (Facsimile Musica Rara, 1967.)

Sadie, Stanley (editor). *The New Grove Dictionary of Musical Instruments*. Macmillan, 1984.

Welch, Christopher. *History of the Boehm Flute*. Rudall Carte, 1896.

PLACES TO VISIT

GREAT BRITAIN

The Bate Collection of Historical Instruments, Faculty of Music, St Aldate's, Oxfo
OX1 1DB. Telephone: 0865 276139.

Edinburgh University Collection of Historic Musical Instruments, Reid Concert Ha
Bristo Square, Edinburgh EH8 9AG. Telephone: 031-667 1011, extension 2573.

The Horniman Museum and Library, London Road, Forest Hill, London SE23 3PC
Telephone: 081-699 2339.

The Royal College of Music, Instrument Museum, Prince Consort Road, South Ke
sington, London SW7 2BS. Telephone: 071-589 3643, extension 346.

The Victoria and Albert Museum, Cromwell Road, South Kensington, Londc
SW7 2RL. Telephone: 071-938 8500.

AUSTRIA

Kunsthistorisches Museum, Sammlung alter Musikinstrument, Neue Burg, A-10l
Vienna.

Salzburger Museum Carolino Augusteum, Museumsplatz 6, A-5010 Salzburg.

BELGIUM

Musée Instrumental du Conservatoire Royal de Musique, Rue Montagne de la Cou
B-1000 Brussels.

FRANCE

Musée Instrumental du Conservatoire National Supérieur de Musique, 14 Rue d
Madrid, F-75008 Paris.

GERMANY

Bayerische Nationalmuseum, Prinzregentenstrasse 3, D-8000 Munich 22.

Deutsche Museum, Museuminsel 1, D-8000 Munich 26.

Germanisches Nationalmuseum (Sammlung Historischer Musikinstrumente), Kartäuser-
gasse 1, D-8500 Nuremburg 11.

*Musikinstrumenten Museum, Staatliches Institut für Musikforschung, Preussischer
Kulturbesitz*, Tiergartenstrasse 1, D-1000 Berlin 30.

Musikinstrumenten-Museum der Karl-Marx-Universität, Täubchenweg 2c-e, DDR-701
Leipzig.

ITALY

Conservatorio di Musica Luigi Cherubini, Museo degli Strumenti Musicali, Piazetta della
Bella Arti 2, I-50100 Florence.

NETHERLANDS

Haags Gemeentemuseum, Stadhouderslaan 41, NL-2517 HV The Hague.

UNITED STATES OF AMERICA

Museum of Fine Arts, Huntington Avenue, Boston, Massachusetts 02115.

Metropolitan Museum of Art, Fifth Avenue at 82nd Street, New York, NY 10028.

Shrine to Music Museum, 414 East Clark Street, Vermillion, South Dakota 57069.

*Smithsonian Institution, National Museum of History and Technology, Division of Mus-
ical Instruments*, Constitution Avenue, Washington, DC 20560.

The Library of Congress (Dayton Miller Collection), 10 First Street SE, Washington,
DC 20540.

USSR

Museum of Musical Instruments, Institute of Theatre, Music and Cinema, 5 St Isaac's
Square, 190000 Leningrad.